Crochet Dreamcatchers
10 Beautiful Patterns for You to Try

Table of contents

Introduction 3
Chapter 1 – Getting Started 5
   Beautiful Baby Dream Catchers 5
   Elegant Shell Dream Catchers 8
Chapter 2 – Unique Catchers for Everyone 11
   Wrist Dreams 11
   The Bluest Dreams Catcher 14
Chapter 3 – For the Kids 17
   Pretty Little Princess Dreams 17
   Simple Beaded Dream Catcher 20
Chapter 4 – Jewels and Things 23
   Hidden Gem Dream Catcher 23
   Blue Beaded Dream Catcher 26
Chapter 5 – Dreams for Around the World 29
   Catching Dreams on the Road 29
   Elegant Catchers 31
Conclusion 34

Introduction

Everyone loves the idea of a dream catcher. There's just something so mystical and captivating about the idea of a dream catcher, it really doesn't matter what you do in life, you simply must have one.

But when it comes to finding the right one, you have to be careful. There are so many of them out there, and you don't just want any random piece. You want something that's going to look great, feel great, and be great in any room you put it in, and that can be a challenge.

There are so many mass produced pieces out there, it's hard to find the one that works for you, simply because it does. That is, until now. If you want to find the right dream catcher, you have to find the one that's perfect for what you need. But how are you supposed to get that unless you are the one who makes it?

How are you going to find the catcher you are dreaming of unless you are the one who puts it together. But aren't dream catchers hard to make? Don't they require all kinds of skill that you don't have? Don't you have to be careful of the method you use, or they aren't going to turn out?

When it comes to making your own dream catchers, there are so many questions that fill your mind. You want something that's going to turn out, but you also want something that's going to be what you want it to be. There's so much more to the story than something that simply looks like a dream catcher, and it can be hard to capture if you are doing it yourself.

That is, until you found this book. With this book, you have everything you need to make the dreamcatcher you have been dreaming of. The one that makes you feel the happiest, the one that brings you the best feeling, and the one you know is going to look great in the corner of the house where you place it. When you make your own dreamcatchers, you are sure to get the one you want, when you want it.

Let me show you the secret of dream catchers, and how you can make your own. There's no end to the ways you can express your creativity, and with the directions you find in this book, you will be making your own in no time.

Let me open the door to a whole new hobby that is going to change your life, and fall in love with your ability to make dream catchers. You aren't ever going to go back to the old way of doing things again.

Dream on.

Chapter 1 – Getting Started

Beautiful Baby Dream Catchers

https://www.flickr.com/photos/stevenleonti/4692178435/in/photolist-89CDbc-ozNze9-r46CKA-7euQvc-dP8tKX-76Ak4W-7WnRTB-729G0e-bg3b7e-0kJS-cpTSE3-71W1jN-6bB8S4-apjZbf-5LiKdi-5NNeZa-6zuiJt-4eJWXr-prtAJ-dGj3Bn-BkNvG-9t7rcq-ascWjc-b0gjUR-88YRtf-HQ4hjH-8GuUaB-9nFawe-fftcXV-4zGTAL-dUwkox-7Wr8cJ-5ruNbq-6kTo1m-HT0BDU-c9fq9y-980Aar-f7Mu1M-dV9XQw-q5g4wZ-H1B5Gb-99U31P-cMwkpd-6CLHZe-7MYScM-9YEZUz-6tYGqJ-a63Wbw-avFE1u-nugzqr

What you will need:

Beads

Thread

Crochet hook

Catcher band

Feathers

Directions:

Use your crochet hook and chain 5. Join with a slip stitch to form a ring, and single crochet in the center of this ring 10 times. Join with a slip stitch.

Chain 1, turn, and single crochet around in the other direction. Chain 1, turn, and single crochet back around. Continue to do this for another 3 or 4 rows. Join with a slip stitch.

For the next row, chain 10, and skip the next 5 stitches, then join with a slip stitch. Chain 10, and skip the next 5 stitches, and join with a slip stitch. Chain 10, and skip the next 5 stitches, then join with a slip stitch. Continue to do this all around.

For the next row, you are going to chain 8, and join with a slip stitch to the top of the chain space. Chain 8, and join with a slip stitch to the top of the chain space. Repeat this around. when you have returned to the beginning, set aside.

Take your ring now, and some yarn (or cord, if that's what you are using). Begin wrapping this around the loop, holding the pieces securely against each other. You want this to be tight, but you also want to center the middle of the catcher in the center of the loop space.

Adjust as you go along, continuously wrapping until you have effectively wrapped around the entire piece. When you get back to the beginning, tie off.

Next, take a length of cord with seed beads, or simply use a length of cord that is colored a variety of colors. This is going to be the outer ring of the dreamcatcher. Wrap this around securely as well, leaving no spaces in between the wraps. It's going to take you a while to complete this, so don't rush the process.

When you get back to the beginning, tie off, and you are ready to add on the tail.

To assemble:

Start by assembling the tails of the catchers before you attach them to the main body of the piece. I prefer to add any beads first, then attach the feathers or knots at the end.

This is the time you really can let your imagination run wild, and have fun with the results. Try adding various lengths and amounts of tails to your catchers, and make every catcher as unique as the dream it chases!

ElegantShellDreamCatchers

https://www.flickr.com/photos/garryknight/3138918348/in/photolist-5MnM4S-nz4ihC-49faV-okJS-92yJmb-fV3zHo-bawgLt-75SBXN-7hj7ap-6EXb6S-aRVLDx-dwjkz6-6paP2q-iVavmi-6p6E92-g52CC6-6p6DYT-bnEsWv-Dj5Z4u-7uswRL-bkaGzL-4YNTET-7yzj2k-7Z9PZ5-qdHsCH-EdHR61-dUFkpN-dGj3Bn-5gqTBK-aj8rAY-5Di6LD-djmxDt-NfHXw-dLiUDw-7mbaSz-4UGcbg-6EQKqT-5pXowy-7xN8qb-a69eHG-6Mrmx3-3ZAVsF-7mbaGt-GrLQD-4XAGq3-sLdM1-6koZUV-grq6nw-4yJyS7-6dS7mQ

What you will need:

Beads

Thread

Shells

Crochet hook

Catcher band

Feathers

Directions:

Use your crochet hook and chain 5. Join with a slip stitch to form a ring, and single crochet in the center of this ring 10 times. Join with a slip stitch.

Chain 1, turn, and single crochet around in the other direction. Chain 1, turn, and single crochet back around. Continue to do this for another 3 or 4 rows. Join with a slip stitch.

For the next row, chain 10, and skip the next 5 stitches, then join with a slip stitch. Chain 10, and skip the next 5 stitches, and join with a slip stitch. Chain 10, and skip the next 5 stitches, then join with a slip stitch. Continue to do this all around.

Tie off, and grab your length of cord.

Hook this cord around the loop, you don't have to make it perfect, just keep it taught. You are going to use these lengths of cord to hold the centerpiece to the outer ring. Before you tie in place, string shells to the length.

Tie off, and move on to the next piece. Space all lengths evenly, using 1 per bump on the initial piece.

Take your ring now, and some yarn (or cord, if that's what you are using). Begin wrapping this around the loop, holding the pieces securely against each other. You want this to be tight, but you also want to center the middle of the catcher in the center of the loop space.

Adjust as you go along, continuously wrapping until you have effectively wrapped around the entire piece. When you get back to the beginning, tie off.

Next, take a length of cord with seed beads, or simply use a length of cord that is colored a variety of colors. This is going to be the outer ring of the dreamcatcher. Wrap this around securely as well, leaving no spaces in between the wraps. It's going to take you a while to complete this, so don't rush the process.

When you get back to the beginning, tie off, and you are ready to add on the tail.

To assemble:

Start by assembling the tails of the catchers before you attach them to the main body of the piece. I prefer to add any beads first, then attach the feathers or knots at the end.

This is the time you really can let your imagination run wild, and have fun with the results. Try adding various lengths and amounts of tails to your catchers, and make every catcher as unique as the dream it chases!

Chapter 2 – Unique Catchers for Everyone

Wrist Dreams

https://www.flickr.com/photos/misadventuresofmaja/13225189814/in/photolist-m9Eyb3-ar3e1B-apgxRx-apjqSm-apfNN6-apfM3P-apjDkC-apgQP8-apixAs-apip7G-apjYsS-aph7GF-apgnbT-apgKdB-apgPZP-apjsdE-2uFWb9-aph3LX-apjMu3-aph2cc-apgKTc-apg1N2-apg9jX-2aeAKH-apj69N-apis2Y-aphe18-apjfts-bSkSAK-aphPRb-apizAs-apgCh2-aphaR4-aph5kp-apjjZJ-apjj9f-aphwdr-apiqYE-9ScRL7-apjC8A-apjKZ4-apgqUn-apjfTd-apjmsh-apj82s-apiwd3-apjPay-apfxnn-aph1yV-apgpic

What you will need:

Beads

Thread

Crochet hook

Catcher band

Feathers

Directions:

To begin, wrap your band securely in the color you want your piece to be, then set aside.

Use the cord now, and wrap it around one point of the loop. Bring it down and around the base of the loop, then bring it up and around the top. You are going to use a braided, criss cross pattern to cross the piece over itself, creating almost a star shape in the center of the piece.

Use the photo as a reference, and continue to work. You want this piece to be simple, and when you are happy with the overall look, tie it off. You now have a mesh piece set in the center of this band.

You are now ready for the strip to secure it in place around your wrist.

Take your crochet hook now, and chain 8. Single crochet across the row, chain 1, turn, and single crochet back to the other side, chain 1, turn, and single crochet across the row.

Chain 1, turn, and single crochet back to the other side. You are going to continue with this pattern now until the strip you have can reach around your wrist, with the center open piece the right size to fit around your dream catcher.

You can make this a little larger to allow for putting the bracelet on or off, but this is up to you.

To assemble:

Once you have the band and the face of the catcher, you are ready to pull it all together. I prefer to make the band loose enough to stretch and fit over my wrist, but you can make this as narrow or as wide as you want it to be.

Attach a button or a snap, or try tying them in place. Now is the time to let your creativity run wild, so have fun with it and see what you come up with.

You could even add miniature tails to the end of the catchers if you like... let your imagination run wild and see what you can create!

TheBluestDreamsCatcher

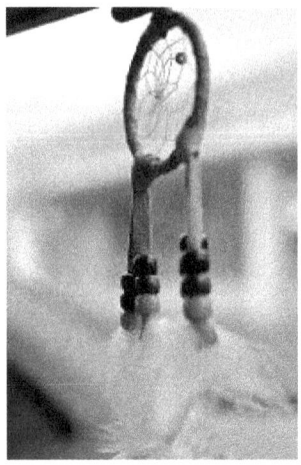

https://www.flickr.com/photos/kosabe/4001421040/in/photolist-76Ak4W-7WnRTB-729G0e-bg3b7e-okJS-cpTSE3-71W1jN-6bB8S4-apjZbf-5LiKdi-5NNeZa-6zuiJt-4eJWXr-prtAJ-dGj3Bn-BkNvG-9t7rcq-ascWjc-bogjUR-88YRtf-HQ4hjH-8GuUaB-9nFawe-fftcXV-4zGTAL-dUwkox-7Wr8cJ-5ruNbq-6kTo1m-HT0BDU-c9fq9y-980Aar-f7Mu1M-dV9XQw-q5g4wZ-H1B5Gb-99U31P-cMwkpd-6CLHZe-7MYScM-9YEZUz-6tYGqJ-a63Wbw-avFE1u-nugzqr-7tShhn-Ee3aP6-aBHPg-eaWUfA-dDAyvg

What you will need:

Beads

Thread

Crochet hook

Catcher band

Feathers

Directions:

Use the cord now, and wrap it around one point of the loop. Bring it down and around the base of the loop, then bring it up and around the top. You are going to use a braided, criss cross pattern to cross the piece over itself, creating almost a star shape in the center of the piece.

Use the photo as a reference, and continue to work. I find it easier to do this with a crochet hook than with my hands, and I am always careful to choose just the right place for the bead on the off center mark.

For this piece, you are working in more of a webbed pattern, so continue to wrap and work at it until you are happy with the overall look of the piece. Don't rush these things take time.

Work with the frame, and not against it, using your crochet hook to loop and twist the piece. Once all is secure, tie off.

Take your ring now, and some yarn (or cord, if that's what you are using). Begin wrapping this around the loop, holding the pieces securely against each other. You want this to be tight, but you also want to center the middle of the catcher in the center of the loop space.

Adjust as you go along, continuously wrapping until you have effectively wrapped around the entire piece. When you get back to the beginning, tie off.

Next, take a length of cord with seed beads, or simply use a length of cord that is colored a variety of colors. This is going to be the outer ring of the dreamcatcher.

Wrap this around securely as well, leaving no spaces in between the wraps. It's going to take you a while to complete this, so don't rush the process.

When you get back to the beginning, tie off, and you are ready to add on the tail.

To assemble:

Start by assembling the tails of the catchers before you attach them to the main body of the piece. I prefer to add any beads first, then attach the feathers or knots at the end.

This is the time you really can let your imagination run wild, and have fun with the results. Try adding various lengths and amounts of tails to your catchers, and make every catcher as unique as the dream it chases!

Chapter 3 – For the Kids

Pretty Little Princess Dreams

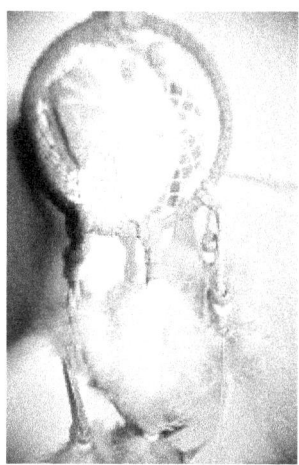

https://www.flickr.com/photos/jacky_oh_yeah/3301857095/in/photolist-62LT5B-5tgFM7-9ZtP0W-3YKVDX-66DRQj-9ZVod9-9RrfbR-66DR0J-jir2XJ-6aNwF5-dAwd48-66zwRc-8XqCp4-66zyzB-98oA8r-9Rre1M-8LM9MQ-7MYScM-a5bTXq-98rKpC-4ima35-pa5bxz-4vwtW6-YwWt-7T7q3k-p6v6tJ-KnC7B-65LwUP-6Qi57N-9odukk-v2UVU-atLWN4-5MnM4S-nz4ihC-axPaGn-49faV-0kJS-92yJmb-fV3zH0-5ofCsN-bawgLt-75SBXN-7hj7ap-6EXb6S-aRVLDx-dwjkz6-6paP2q-iVavmi-6p6E92-g52CC6

What you will need:

Beads

Thread

Crochet hook

Catcher band

Feathers

Directions:

Use the cord, and wrap it around one point of the loop. Bring it down and around the base of the loop, then bring it up and around the top. You are going to use a braided, criss cross pattern to cross the piece over itself, creating almost a star shape in the center of the piece.

Use the photo as a reference, and continue to work. I find it easier to do this with a crochet hook than with my hands, and I am always careful to choose just the right place for the bead on the off center mark.

For this piece, you are working in more of a webbed pattern, so continue to wrap and work at it until you are happy with the overall look of the piece. Don't rush these things take time.

Work with the frame, and not against it, using your crochet hook to loop and twist the piece. Once all is secure, tie off.

Take your ring now, and some yarn (or cord, if that's what you are using). Begin wrapping this around the loop, holding the pieces securely against each other. You want this to be tight, but you also want to center the middle of the catcher in the center of the loop space.

Adjust as you go along, continuously wrapping until you have effectively wrapped around the entire piece. When you get back to the beginning, tie off.

Next, take a length of cord with seed beads, or simply use a length of cord that is colored a variety of colors. This is going to be the outer ring of the dreamcatcher. Wrap this around securely as well, leaving no spaces in between the wraps. It's going to take you a while to complete this, so don't rush the process.

When you get back to the beginning, tie off, and you are ready to add on the tail.

To assemble:

Start by assembling the tails of the catchers before you attach them to the main body of the piece. I prefer to add any beads first, then attach the feathers or knots at the end.

This is the time you really can let your imagination run wild, and have fun with the results. Try adding various lengths and amounts of tails to your catchers, and make every catcher as unique as the dream it chases!

SimpleBeadedDreamCatcher

https://www.flickr.com/photos/tillwe/35558055/in/photolist-49faV-9kJS-92yJmb-fV3zHo-5ofCsN-bawgLt-75SBXN-7hj7ap-6EXb6S-aRVLDx-dwjkz6-6paP2q-iVavmi-6p6E92-g52CC6-6p6DYT-bnEsWv-Dj5Z4u-7uswRL-9DBtbk-bk4GzL-4YNTET-7yzj2k-3eXcGB-anaepA-7Z9PZ5-6L6h66-qdHsCH-4NgD4b-EdHR61-dUFkpN-dGj3Bn-5gqTBK-sLdM1-6koZUV-grq6nw-4yJyS7-aj8rAY-6dS7mQ-5Di6LD-djmxDt-eqvjLk-6paNSU-8H7BRQ-6ET24B-6MzZ7B-cBZAhS-bc1AZc-99X9qy-7eBPzN

What you will need:

Beads

Thread

Crochet hook

Catcher band

Feathers

Directions:

Use a multi-colored thread for this piece. You can also string seed beads to the piece, but I prefer to use multi-colored thread.

Start by wrapping the cord around your loop. Bring it down and around the base of the loop, then bring it up and around the top. You are going to use a braided, criss cross pattern to cross the piece over itself, creating almost a star shape in the center of the piece.

Use the photo as a reference, and continue to work. I find it easier to do this with a crochet hook than with my hands, but you can do what feels right for you.

For this piece, you are working in more of a webbed pattern, so continue to wrap and work at it until you are happy with the overall look of the piece. Don't rush these things take time.

Work with the frame, and not against it, using your crochet hook to loop and twist the piece. Once all is secure, tie off.

Take your ring now, and some yarn (or cord, if that's what you are using). Begin wrapping this around the loop, holding the pieces securely against each other. You want this to be tight, but you also want to center the middle of the catcher in the center of the loop space.

Adjust as you go along, continuously wrapping until you have effectively wrapped around the entire piece. When you get back to the beginning, tie off.

Next, take a length of cord with seed beads, or simply use a length of cord that is colored a variety of colors. This is going to be the outer ring of the dreamcatcher. Wrap this around securely as well, leaving no spaces in between the wraps. It's going to take you a while to complete this, so don't rush the process.

When you get back to the beginning, tie off, and you are ready to add on the tail.

To assemble:

Start by assembling the tails of the catchers before you attach them to the main body of the piece. I prefer to add any beads first, then attach the feathers or knots at the end.

This is the time you really can let your imagination run wild, and have fun with the results. Try adding various lengths and amounts of tails to your catchers, and make every catcher as unique as the dream it chases!

Chapter 4 – Jewels and Things

Hidden Gem Dream Catcher

https://www.flickr.com/photos/carterpino/1471302852/in/photolist-3f1P5y-5mmzVa-6FGePv-3f2Ag7-6Y3LU3-hMVcn-3f1Q4J-ppKUyk-BZdz3-5XqnpX-6hJhrz-5XSc9T-67pwaP-e6LbKc-5TYec5-xFZfTw-dB9j2z-6hJhuT-6hNrNJ-dRFWdF-7Z5RAR-62LT5B-5tgFM7-9ZtPoW-3YKVDX-66DRQj-9ZVod9-9RrfbR-66DRoJ-iir2XJ-6aNwF5-dAwd48-66zwRc-8XqCp4-66zyzB-980A8r-9Rre1M-8LM9MQ-7MYScM-a5bTXq-98rKpC-4ima35-pa5bxz-4vw1W6-YwWt-7T7q3k-p6v6tJ-KnC7B-65LwUP-6Qi57N

What you will need:

Beads

Thread

Crochet hook

Catcher band

Feathers

Stones

Directions:

Use the cord, and wrap it around one point of the loop. You are going to work this around the stone centerpiece in the middle of the catcher, so focus on that being your focal point.

All webbing is going to be made around this stone, and you will do your best to keep the outer ends even.

Bring this cord down and around the base of the loop, then bring it up and around the top. You are going to use a braided, criss cross pattern to cross the piece over itself, creating almost a star shape in the center of the piece.

Use the photo as a reference, and continue to work. I find it easier to do this with a crochet hook than with my hands, and I am always careful to choose just the right place for the bead on the off center mark.

For this piece, you are working in more of a webbed pattern, so continue to wrap and work at it until you are happy with the overall look of the piece. Don't rush these things take time.

Work with the frame, and not against it, using your crochet hook to loop and twist the piece. Once all is secure, tie off.

Take your ring now, and some yarn (or cord, if that's what you are using). Begin wrapping this around the loop, holding the pieces securely against each other. You want this to be tight, but you also want to center the middle of the catcher in the center of the loop space.

Adjust as you go along, continuously wrapping until you have effectively wrapped around the entire piece. When you get back to the beginning, tie off.

Next, take a length of cord with seed beads, or simply use a length of cord that is colored a variety of colors. This is going to be the outer ring of the dreamcatcher. Wrap this around securely as well, leaving no spaces in between the wraps. It's going to take you a while to complete this, so don't rush the process.

When you get back to the beginning, tie off, and you are ready to add on the tail.

To assemble:

Start by assembling the tails of the catchers before you attach them to the main body of the piece. I prefer to add any beads first, then attach the feathers or knots at the end.

This is the time you really can let your imagination run wild, and have fun with the results. Try adding various lengths and amounts of tails to your catchers, and make every catcher as unique as the dream it chases!

BlueBeadedDreamCatcher

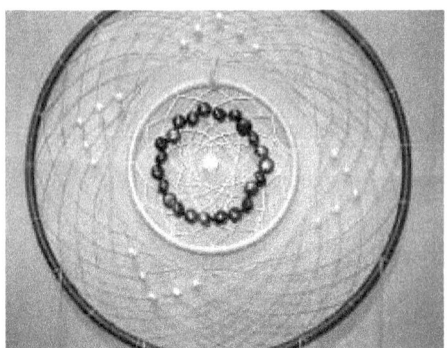

https://www.flickr.com/photos/15442697@N06/3920777278/in/photolist-5pXowy-7xN8qb-9h8v7V-ei79ND-6Yt1uf-5WYZ8d-a69eHG-6cdcTe-8U1Gx1-o1J4mz-56RXGu-74VUpH-6Mrmx3-5VXCZx-Nyjca-6AHX9x-bVrsFm-6LcENE-83hHwt-8zSK1k-4YTauy-qQhjEm-6YoZdi-3ZAVsF-9Xw8Tc-6Yt1oS-aVHJ2-eicW7E-575Bz5-GrMu2-6PKpsp-aBHPg-6AmUh4-GrGr3-6opmwN-5Waf9V-aDojCb-GrMJF-6wG4bA-7mbaGt-5WexyS-5Waf5K-GrLQD-GrMsn-3Pe4yc-4XAGq3-GrGnG-6Qva3b-GrLQ4-GrMvx

What you will need:

Beads

Thread

Crochet hook

Catcher band

Feathers

Directions:

This catcher is worked in 2 parts. First, complete the sequence for the inner catcher, then repeat for the outer.

For the first:

Use the cord, and wrap it around one point of the loop. Bring it down and around the base of the loop, then bring it up and around the top. You are going to use a braided, criss cross pattern to cross the piece over itself, creating almost a star shape in the center of the piece.

You will work with a lot of beads on this one. There are going to be a lot of beads on the inside, then a lot more on the outer edge. Do what feels right.

Use the photo as a reference, and continue to work. I find it easier to do this with a crochet hook than with my hands, so I can choose right where I want to place each bead.

For this piece, you are working in more of a webbed pattern, so continue to wrap and work at it until you are happy with the overall look of the piece. Don't rush these things take time.

Work with the frame, and not against it, using your crochet hook to loop and twist the piece. Once all is secure, tie off.

Take your ring now, and some yarn (or cord, if that's what you are using). Begin wrapping this around the loop, holding the pieces securely against each other. You want this to be tight, but you also want to center the middle of the catcher in the center of the loop space.

Adjust as you go along, continuously wrapping until you have effectively wrapped around the entire piece. When you get back to the beginning, tie off.

Next, take a length of cord with seed beads, or simply use a length of cord that is colored a variety of colors. This is going to be the outer ring of the dreamcatcher. Wrap this around securely as well, leaving no spaces in between the wraps. It's going to take you a while to complete this, so don't rush the process.

Repeat it all for the second, then bring together as you see in the photo.

When you get back to the beginning, tie off, and you are ready to add on the tail.

To assemble:

Start by assembling the tails of the catchers before you attach them to the main body of the piece. I prefer to add any beads first, then attach the feathers or knots at the end.

This is the time you really can let your imagination run wild, and have fun with the results. Try adding various lengths and amounts of tails to your catchers, and make every catcher as unique as the dream it chases!

Chapter 5 – Dreams for Around the World

CatchingDreamsontheRoad

https://www.flickr.com/photos/flyone1106/190022927/in/photolist-hMVcn-3f1Q4J-ppKUyk-BZdz3-5XqnpX-6hJhrz-5XSc9T-67pwaP-e6LbKc-5TYec5-xFZfTw-dB9i2z-6hJhuT-6hNrNJ-dRFWdF-7Z5RAR-62LT5B-5tgFM7-9ZtPoW-3YKVDX-66DRQj-9ZVod9-9RrfbR-66DRoJ-iir2XJ-6aNwF5-dAwd48-66zwRc-8XqCp4-66zyzB-980A8r-9Rre1M-8LM9MQ-7MYScM-a5bTXq-98rKpC-4ima35-pa5bxz-4vwtW6-YwWt-7T7q3k-p6v6tJ-KnC7B-65LwUP-6Qi57N-9odukk-v2UVU-atLWN4-5MnM4S-nz4jhC

What you will need:

Beads

Thread

Crochet hook

Catcher band

Feathers

Directions:

Start with the cord, and wrap it around one point of the loop. Bring it down and around the base of the loop, then bring it up and around the top. You are going to use a braided, criss cross pattern to cross the piece over itself, creating almost a star shape in the center of the piece.

Use the photo as a reference, and continue to work. You want this piece to be simple, and when you are happy with the overall look, tie it off. You now have a mesh piece set in the center of this band.

Take your ring now, and some yarn (or cord, if that's what you are using). Begin wrapping this around the loop, holding the pieces securely against each other. You want this to be tight, but you also want to center the middle of the catcher in the center of the loop space.

Adjust as you go along, continuously wrapping until you have effectively wrapped around the entire piece. When you get back to the beginning, tie off.

Next, take a length of cord with seed beads, or simply use a length of cord that is colored a variety of colors. This is going to be the outer ring of the dreamcatcher. Wrap this around securely as well, leaving no spaces in between the wraps. It's going to take you a while to complete this, so don't rush the process.

When you get back to the beginning, tie off, and you are ready to add on the tail.

To assemble:

Start by assembling the tails of the catchers before you attach them to the main body of the piece. I prefer to add any beads first, then attach the feathers or knots at the end.

This is the time you really can let your imagination run wild, and have fun with the results. Try adding various lengths and amounts of tails to your catchers, and make every catcher as unique as the dream it chases!

ElegantCatchers

https://www.flickr.com/photos/129047484@N07/20799574620/in/photolist-xFZfTw-dB9j2z-6bJhuT-6bNrNJ-dREWdF-7Z5RAR-62LT5B-5tgFM7-9ZtP0W-3YKVDX-66DRQj-9ZV9d9-9RrfbR-66DRoJ-ijr2XJ-6aNwF5-dAwd48-66zwRc-8XqCp4-66zyzB-980A8r-9Rre1M-8LM9MQ-7MYScM-a5bTXq-98rKpC-4ima35-pa5bxz-4vwtW6-YwWt-7T7q3k-p6v6tJ-KnC7B-65LwUP-6Qj57N-9odukk-v2UVU-atLWN4-5MnM4S-nz4ihC-axPaGn-49faV-okJS-92yJmb-fV3zHo-50fCsN-bawgLt-75SBXN-7hj7ap-6EXb6S

What you will need:

Beads

Thread

Crochet hook

Catcher band

Feathers

Directions:

Use the cord to create a thick weave with this one. Take your time, it's going to be worth it when you are done.

Bring it down and around the base of the loop, then bring it up and around the top. You are going to use a braided, criss cross pattern to cross the piece over itself, creating almost a star shape in the center of the piece.

For this piece, you are working in more of a webbed pattern, so continue to wrap and work at it until you are happy with the overall look of the piece. Don't rush these things take time. Use the photo as reference for what you are doing.

Work with the frame, and not against it, using your crochet hook to loop and twist the piece. Once all is secure, tie off.

Take your ring now, and some yarn (or cord, if that's what you are using). Begin wrapping this around the loop, holding the pieces securely against each other.

You want this to be tight, but you also want to center the middle of the catcher in the center of the loop space.

Adjust as you go along, continuously wrapping until you have effectively wrapped around the entire piece. When you get back to the beginning, tie off.

Next, take a length of cord with seed beads, or simply use a length of cord that is colored a variety of colors. This is going to be the outer ring of the dreamcatcher. Wrap this around securely as well, leaving no spaces in between the wraps. It's going to take you a while to complete this, so don't rush the process.

When you get back to the beginning, tie off, and you are ready to add on the tail.

To assemble:

Start by assembling the tails of the catchers before you attach them to the main body of the piece. I prefer to add any beads first, then attach the feathers or knots at the end.

This is the time you really can let your imagination run wild, and have fun with the results. Try adding various lengths and amounts of tails to your catchers, and make every catcher as unique as the dream it chases!

Conclusion

There you have it, everything you need to know about dream catchers, and how you can use crochet to make them yourself. There's so many different ways you can make these wonderful accent pieces for your home, and it really doesn't matter what your preferred method if, if you want to make one, you can do it.

I hope this book was able to inspire you to create your very own dream catchers, and to express yourself in ways you haven't before. With this book, you are going to see just how easy it is to create any piece you want, and to throw in your won flare with each one.

Whether you are making a piece that is small and simple, or if you are working on one that is elegant and full of life, you are going to find what you are looking for with this book. I hope this book inspires you to go bigger, better, and greater than ever, and that you are able to take your dream catching hobby to the next level.

When you are making your own dreamcatchers, you are able to do anything and everything you want. There's no end to the ways you can throw in your own flare to each look, or to what you can do with each piece when you are finished with them.

I hope this book shows you just how easy it is to create your own dreamcatchers, and that you are able to take the inspiration you gain from seeing these projects to make them the way you have dreamed of. There's no end to the possibilities, and the more you throw in the things in life that are important to you, the better off you will be.

With this book, you are going to get the results you want. There's no way you can go wrong when you are able to create them with your own hands, and when you see the results you are hoping to see, you will feel even more creative.

I want this book to inspire you, and open the door to a whole new way of décor. Show appreciation for another culture, fall in love with their values and their way of life, and show the world how you feel about being able to reach for the stars... and catch your dreams.

There's nothing standing in your way, so get out there and go for it.

You know you want to, and you deserve to reach your dreams.

Now get out there, chase your dreams for all your worth, then sit back and relax.

With these accessories around your home, you are going to catch the best of the best.

www.ingramcontent.com/pod-product-compliance
Lightning Source LLC
Chambersburg PA
CBHW061015170325
23604CB00017B/177